BEST FRIEND
IN THE
WORLD

summersdale

BEST FRIEND IN THE WORLD

Summersdale Publishers Ltd
46 West Street
Chichester
West Sussex
PO19 1RP
UK

www.summersdale.com

Printed and bound by Tien Wah Press, Singapore

ISBN: 1-84024-662-6
ISBN 13: 978-1-84024-662-9

BEST FRIEND
IN THE
WORLD

We are all travellers in the wilderness of this world, and the best we can find in our travels is an honest friend.

Robert Louis Stevenson

Friendship is born at that moment when one person says to another, What! You, too? I thought I was the only one.

C. S. Lewis

Each friend represents a world in us, a world possibly not born until they arrive, and it is only by this meeting that a new world is born.

Anaïs Nin

My best friend is the one who brings out the best in me.

Henry Ford

*What joy is better than
news of friends?*

Robert Browning

*There is one friend in the life
of each of us who seems not a
separate person, however dear
and beloved, but an expansion,
an interpretation, of one's self,
the very meaning of one's soul.*

Edith Wharton

*What is a friend? A single
soul in two bodies.*

Aristotle

*What is a friend? I will tell
you... it is someone with whom
you dare to be yourself.*

Frank Crane

*Friendship's a noble name,
'tis love refined.*

Susanna Centlivre

No distance of place or lapse of time can lessen the friendship of those who are thoroughly persuaded of each other's worth.

Robert Southey

It's the friends you can call up at 4 a.m. that matter.

Marlene Dietrich

We would build on a sure foundation in friendship, we must love our friends for their sakes rather than for our own.

Charlotte Brontë

*Friendship is the golden thread
that ties the heart of all the world.*

John Evelyn

*Friendship is the only
rose without thorns.*

Madeleine de Scudéry

*Friends are relatives you
make for yourself.*

Eustache Deschamps

A friend is one who believes
in you when you have ceased
to believe in yourself.

Anonymous

Many kinds of fruit grow upon the tree of life, but none so sweet as friendship.

Lucy Larcom

Your friend is the man who knows all about you, and still likes you.

Elbert Hubbard

*Friends are those rare people
who ask how we are and then
wait to hear the answer.*

Ed Cunningham

A friend is like a rainbow. They brighten your life when you've been through a storm.

Anonymous

We have been friends together,
In sunshine and in shade.

Caroline Norton

*The most beautiful discovery
that true friends can make is
that they can grow separately
without growing apart.*

Elizabeth Foley

*A real friend will tell you when you
have spinach stuck in your teeth.*

Anonymous

*Show me your best friend and
I'll tell you who you are.*

Russian proverb

Trouble is a sieve through which we sift our acquaintances. Those too big to pass through are our friends.

Arlene Francis

A friend is a gift you give yourself.

Robert Louis Stevenson

True friends not only protect you from others when something goes bad, but from yourself when you try to take blame.

Anonymous

*True friendship is like sound
health; the value of it is seldom
known until it be lost.*

Charles Caleb Colton

*The most called upon prerequisite
of a friend is an accessible ear.*

Maya Angelou

Two may talk together under the same roof for many years, yet never really meet; and two others at first speech are old friends.

Mary Catherwood

No love, no friendship, can cross the path of our destiny without leaving some mark on it forever.

François Mauriac

Remember that the most valuable antiques are dear old friends.

H. Jackson Brown, Jr

Every man should have a fair-sized cemetery in which to bury the faults of his friends.

Henry Brooks Adams

The proper office of a friend is to side with you when you are in the wrong. Nearly anybody will side with you when you are in the right.

Mark Twain

Where there are friends,
there is wealth.

Plautus

Perhaps the most delightful friendships are those in which there is much agreement, much disputation, and yet more personal liking.

George Eliot

Certain flaws are necessary for the whole. It would seem strange if old friends lacked certain quirks.

Johann Wolfgang von Goethe

Friends are like melons. Shall I tell you why? To find one good you must one hundred try.

Claude Mermet

Friendship is certainly the finest balm for the pangs of disappointed love.

Jane Austen

*The best way to keep your friends
is not to give them away.*

Wilson Mizner

Never forget the days I spent with you. Continue to be my friend, as you will always find me yours.

Ludwig van Beethoven

Let's face it, friends make life a lot more fun.

Charles R. Swindoll

Without friends no one would choose to live, though he had all other goods.

Aristotle

*Friendship is the hardest thing
in the world to explain.*

Muhammad Ali

A true friend is someone who thinks that you are a good egg even though he knows that you are slightly cracked.

Bernard Meltzer

*The better part of one's life
consists of his friendships.*

Abraham Lincoln

The finest kind of friendship is between two people who expect a great deal of each other, but never ask it.

Sylvia Bremer

Friendship is a word, the very sight of which in print makes the heart warm.

Augustine Birrell

We cannot tell the precise moment when a friendship is formed. As in filling a vessel drop by drop, there is at last one drop that makes it run over. So in a series of kindnesses there is at last one drop that makes the heart run over.

Samuel Johnson

Walking with a friend in the dark is better than walking alone in the light.

Helen Keller

Treat your friends like your pictures and put them in your best light.

Jennie Jerome Churchill

Nothing opens the heart like a true friend, to whom you may impart griefs, joys, fears, hopes... and whatever lies upon the heart.

Francis Bacon

O friend, my bosom said,
Through thee alone the sky is arched,
Through thee the rose is red,
All things through thee
take nobler form...

Ralph Waldo Emerson

The best mirror is an old friend.

George Herbert

*The most I can do for my friend
is simply to be his friend. I have
no wealth to bestow on him. If he
knows that I am happy in loving
him, he will want no other reward.
Is not friendship divine in this?*

Henry David Thoreau

*Friends are like poems, you may
never fully understand them,
but you will always love them.*

Anonymous

*On the road between friends'
houses, grass does not grow.*

Esther M. Clark

*Friendship improves happiness,
and abates misery, by doubling
our joy, and dividing our grief.*

Joseph Addison

Friendship is love with understanding.

Proverb

A friend is someone who knows the song in your heart, and can sing it back to you when you have forgotten the words.

Anonymous

A companion loves some agreeable qualities which a man may possess, but a friend loves the man himself.

James Boswell

A good friend is like an oasis in the desert.

Old Chinese proverb

*'Stay' is a charming word
in a friend's vocabulary.*

Louisa May Alcott

I no doubt deserved my enemies, but I don't believe I deserved my friends.

Walt Whitman

It takes a long time to grow an old friend.

John Leonard

A friend is one who walks in when others walk out.

Walter Winchell

There is nothing on this earth to be more prized than true friendship.

Saint Thomas Aquinas

www.summersdale.com